D0679818

TOASTS
&
TRIBUTES

OTHER GENTLEMANNERS™ BOOKS

TOASTS
&
TRIBUTES

REVISED AND EXPANDED

....

A GENTLEMAN'S GUIDE TO PERSONAL CORRESPONDENCE AND THE NOBLE TRADITION OF THE TOAST

JOHN BRIDGES
AND BRYAN CURTIS

THOMAS NELSON
Since 1798

NASHVILLE DALLAS MEXICO CITY RIO DE JANEIRO

Published in Nashville, Tennessee, by Thomas Nelson. Thomas Nelson is a registered trademark of Thomas Nelson, Inc.

Thomas Nelson, Inc., titles may be purchased in bulk for educational, business, fund-raising, or sales promotional use. For information, please e-mail SpecialMarkets@ThomasNelson.com.

ISBN 13: 978-1-4016-0467-7

The Library of Congress has cataloged an earlier edition of this book as follows:

Bridges, John, 1950–
  Toasts & tributes / John Bridges and Bryan Curtis.
      159 p. ; 21 cm.
   ISBN: 1-4016-0232-0
   ISBN: 1-4016-0254-1
   1. Toasts. 2. Letter Writing. 3. Etiquette for Men. I. Curtis, Bryan, 1960– II. Title.
PN6341 .B67 2005   2005276578

Printed in the United States of America

12 13 14 15 16 WOR 6 5 4 3 2 1

*For Jon Glassmeyer and Scott
Ridgway, neither of whom ever lifts
a half-empty glass*

–J.B.

*For Rodney Mitchell, my generous,
talented and very dear friend*

–B.C.

CONTENTS

PREFACE

A gentleman cherishes the memorable moments of his life, both while they are happening and after they are over. When he is called upon to say a few words on a happy occasion, he does his best to choose the words that honor the occasion itself and the people with whom the gentleman shares it. In that way, as he raises his glass to lead a toast, he also raises the spirits of the moment, making them even brighter.

Many times, however, a gentleman wishes to mark the moment by putting his feelings on the page. Sometimes his intention is to say thank you for a lovely evening, a thoughtful gift, or some special kindness shown to him.

At other times his purpose may be to express his concern for the sadness of a beloved friend or a valued coworker. Or he may be seizing the moment to share in the joy of a wedding celebration, the birth of a new baby, or a well-deserved promotion at the office.

Whether he stands at the head of the table with celebratory glass in hand, sits down at his desk with pen and ink and paper, or (on some rarefied occasions) sends along a carefully worded e-mail, a gentleman does his best to give life's important moments the attention they are due.

This book provides a gentleman with the right words—the words he will need to make those moments last. Such moments, after all, are few and far between.

A GENTLEMAN RAISES HIS GLASS

A gentleman's life is full of happy occasions, some of them formal, some of them as easy going as a cookout on a Labor Day afternoon. A gentleman knows that on any of these occasions he and his friends may choose to mark the moment by raising a glass, or a bottle, in honor of a special guest or a treasured colleague. The occasion itself may call for a toast for no other reason than to acknowledge the spirit of the moment and the simple pleasure of being among friends. At such times a gentleman should feel most at ease, since he is only being asked to say what is truly in his heart.

It is at such moments, however, that a gentleman often clinches—particularly if the occasion involves the marriage of his own child, the retirement of a beloved colleague, or his own departure from an organization to which he has given much of himself over a long period. He may also find it difficult to put into words his feelings about the marriage of a long-time friend or the union of two friends whose relationship he has helped nurture.

A gentleman's discomfort may be made greater by the sense that a spotlight is shining in his face. In his heart of hearts, however, a gentleman knows that, if he is the one offering the toast, *he* is not the center of attention. He also knows that he is not expected to wax eloquent or to be quoted in the morning paper. He just says what is in his heart and lets the party proceed.

What follows are some simple guidelines for making toasts, accompanied by some easily adaptable examples. These should not be taken as strict rules that must be followed or as rigid models to be imitated. Rather, they are intended to point the gentleman in the right direction at those times when he chooses to raise his glass and express his respect, admiration, or love for a friend.

A gentleman knows that toasts are intended as tributes and, as such, are a means of celebration.

———

A gentleman knows that a toast need not be epic in length. Usually a few well-thought-out words are more effective than an extended tribute would be.

———

A gentleman knows that the freshest toast of the evening is the first one offered.

———

To make a toast more personal, a gentleman may include reminiscences and anecdotes. However, he makes sure that the entire assembly will appreciate and understand them.

———

A gentleman knows that a toast is not a full-fledged testimonial, outlining the honoree's lifetime achievements and accomplishments.

When a gentleman makes a toast
to someone present in the room, he
makes it *directly* to that person, not to
the table at large.

————

A gentleman knows that he need not
end his toast by saying, "Here's to Tom,"
"Here's to Gloria," or "Here's to the bride
and groom"—although such expressions
are never inappropriate. Simply
extending his glass toward the honoree
is a sufficient conclusion.

————

A gentleman knows that, since
toasts are intended for celebratory
occasions, they require at least
moderately formal glassware.

————

A gentleman knows that, beer steins
excepted, he may not toast with anything
resembling a coffee cup.

A gentleman does not take it upon himself to deliver a toast at a breakfast meeting.

If a gentleman is asked to deliver a toast at a breakfast meeting, or any meeting before noon, he declines by simply saying, "I'd really prefer not to."

If a gentleman is pressed to deliver a toast at an inappropriate moment, he stands his ground, saying, "No. I'd really prefer you'd ask somebody else to do that. I'm not comfortable making a toast at this time."

A gentleman never uses a toast to ridicule or embarrass a friend. Neither does he use a toast as a sentimental excuse to bring a friend or coworker to tears.

A gentleman knows that he must stand to deliver a toast, except when the event is taking place in a crowded public restaurant.

Even in a crowded public restaurant, a gentleman must at least lean forward toward the others at the table before delivering a toast.

———

When a gentleman is delivering a toast to his host or the evening's honoree, he raises his glass to that person and waits for other guests at the table to lift their glasses before he begins his toast. When he has finished delivering the toast, he may wish to share in the clinking of glasses by touching his own glass against that of another guest near him. Once this activity has subsided, he feels free to take a sip from his own glass.

———

Before delivering a toast, a gentleman waits until everyone at his table has at least some wine (or some other liquid) in his or her glass.

A gentleman never initiates a toast until the glasses of all the ladies at his table have been filled.

———

After a toast has been delivered, each guest takes a sip from his or her glass.

———

Knowing that further toasts are likely to follow, a gentleman does not drain his glass after the first tribute has been given.

———

If possible, a gentleman disdains the use of note cards when delivering a toast. Not only are the cards distracting to him and to his listeners, but they may also require the awkward juggling of glassware and cardstock.

A gentleman understands that a toast is a public—or at the very least, a semi-public—gesture. He understands that it is most likely inappropriate at a *tête-à-tête* dinner. If he attempts such a thing, he runs the risk of asking his dinner partner to respond in kind, which boils down to begging for a compliment–pretty much the same thing as asking a friend to say thank you for a thank-you note. Neither of those activities is in any way attractive or socially acceptable.

————

If a gentleman feels that he must propose a toast at a *tête-à-tête* dinner, he says nothing more than "Here's to us" or "Here's to our friendship."

————

A gentleman knows that when he is asked to make a toast he does not seize the opportunity to do stand-up comedy–even if he is by profession a stand-up comic.

When making a toast, a gentleman keeps to the point and remembers that he is on the clock.

————

A gentleman does not take it upon himself to deliver the opening toast unless he is the host of the celebration or has been asked to do so by the host or master of ceremonies.

————

When he is one of a number of scheduled toast-givers, a gentleman does not monopolize the microphone.

————

If in a series of toasts or tributes, a gentleman hears a story he was going to tell or a toast he was going to make, he does not repeat it. He thinks quickly on his feet and composes a new toast if he is capable of doing so. Otherwise, he makes a simple congratulatory toast, knowing he will have other moments to share his feelings with the honoree.

A Gentleman Raises His Glass

A gentleman knows that even at a bachelor party a toast is intended to be a tribute, not an embarrassment.

————

In the spirit of fun, a best man may include ribald remarks in his toast at the bachelor party, but at the rehearsal dinner or wedding reception, he keeps it clean, kindhearted, and concise.

————

Considering the likely emotional impact of the moment, a father of the bride is especially wise to plan his toast carefully, keeping it brief and, to the best of his abilities, convivial.

————

A gentleman knows that a well-planned or well-phrased toast should never last longer than sixty seconds.

A gentleman knows that, even in the most celebratory of circumstances, a toast merely underscores the reason for the celebration and is not the celebration itself.

THE TOASTS

A Toast from the Father of the Bride

"Here's to you, Jack. Maddie has been, and always will be, my treasure. I know you will treasure her too. As her father, I have always loved her and always will. Now, as a friend, I pass that same love along to you."

A Gentleman Does Not Say:

"Here's to you, Jack. If you hurt my little girl, I'll kill you."

A Toast from the Father of the Groom

"Madeline, even when Jack was a little kid, he had a gift for seeking out the best of everything. I remember when we bought his first catcher's mitt. Joanie and I watched while he tried on every single mitt on the wall at Gillespie's Team Sports, searching until he found just the one he wanted. He chose it not only because it was a beautiful mitt but also because, to his way of thinking, it was the one that fit him best, the one he was going to cherish for a lifetime. He's still got that gift for finding the best of everything, and that's what he's found in you.

"Joanie and I welcome you to our family as if you had always been there. Please know you have all our love."

A Gentleman Does Not Say:

"Madeline, I hope you have more luck keeping him in line than I did."

A Toast from the Best Man

"Maddie and Jack, as I watched you exchange your rings during the ceremony, I teared up a little bit. Here was my best friend finally making the commitment to act like a grown-up. But I have to say I was a little envious as well because he was making that commitment to a woman I have come to love and cherish almost as much as if we, too, had played Little League together.

"I am deeply honored to be a part of this day. I wish you endless days like today, every one of them filled with joy."

A Gentleman Does Not Say:

"Jack, who am I going to chase hotties with now that you're off the market?"

A Toast Honoring a Couple Who Have Renewed Their Marriage Vows

"Ted and Sue, today is about two special people I am fortunate to call my friends. I was not a part of your lives twenty-five years ago when you first said, 'I do.' However, as I have gotten to know both of you, I can say that your continued love and commitment to each other is not only reassuring, but it is also inspiring to those of us who are lucky enough to be a part of your lives.

"Here's to Ted and Sue and a wonderful evening."

A Gentleman Does Not Say:

"Ted, you know buddy, you're making the rest of us look bad. It was hard enough for me to do this once. And here you have to go ahead and say 'I do' again."

A Toast Honoring Friends Who Have Been Married Before

"Rachel and Brad, you are people of joy, you are people of wisdom, you are people who know how to value every minute of life. As the two of you come together, joining your families into one great, noisy brood, a whole new family is being formed.

"Thank you for including us in this exciting day."

A Gentleman Does Not Say:

"Rachel, I'm glad you finally came along. If I'd had to meet one more of Brad's girlfriends, I would have hung myself."

The Tradition of the Toast

No one really knows how the traditions of toasting and clinking glasses actually began—or for that matter how the word "toast" came to refer to raising a glass in celebration or tribute—but there are a few popular theories.

The ancient Greeks occasionally liked to settle business disputes by dribbling a little poison in the punch. Offering a toast to good health while raising glasses was considered a gesture of good faith, not to mention that there was less risk of being poisoned if all diners were obliged to sip from their own glasses at the same time. Another theory is that the clinking of glasses acted as a deterrent: a victim's tainted beverage could slosh into the glass of the poisoner.

The term "toast" most likely comes from the ancient Romans, who had the habit of putting burnt bread into their wine. Some believe this was to soften the bread, while others say it was to remove the contaminants from impure wine—thus leading to the custom of drinking to one another's health.

A Clink, Not a Crash

A gentleman would never, of course, slam his champagne flute—or his wine goblet, old-fashioned glass, or iced-tea glass— against his partner's glass so smartly as to cause a shattering collision. He simply touches the rim of his glass against the side of the glass most readily offered him. If breakage occurs, he simply asks for a new glass, since the fault clearly is not his own.

A Toast upon a Milestone Anniversary for a Gentleman's Parents

"Mom and Dad, this is a great party, but it still isn't great enough to demonstrate how much we love the two of you and how grateful we are for all your patience, guidance, and support. You'll notice that I didn't mention your advice since, as you know, most of the time we never took it. But now we know that almost all of the time—except for that time when you wouldn't let me go to Chicago—you were right. In fact, I guess I'd even have to say you were right about Chicago.

"I know the two of you are lucky to have each other. But I just want to say how lucky all of us feel to have you. Mom and Dad, I love you."

A Gentleman Does Not Say:

"I'm so happy Mom ignored Grandpa's warning and eloped with Dad. I guess you showed him."

A Toast upon a Milestone Anniversary for a Gentleman's Friends

"Linda and Grover, it's an honor for us to be here as you celebrate forty years of marriage. You are great partners and great friends. As we've been treated to your generous hospitality over the years, we've watched you working together. I don't think I've seen either of you growl at the other, even when Linda might have needed to say, 'Grover, darling, you know there's *three* days' worth of trash in those bags.'

"You've shared so many of the good times, and this night is one of those good times. Thank you for including us on this special night."

A Gentleman Does Not Say:

"I know there were times when you were close to throwing in the towel, but I speak for everyone here when I say that I'm glad you didn't."

A Toast upon the Birthday of a Close Friend

"Olivia, we've come here to celebrate, not just because it's your birthday but also because you are a dear and cherished friend every day. "Happy birthday, with all our love."

A Gentleman Does Not Say:

"Olivia, you are such a special lady. I can't believe a man hasn't snapped you up yet."

A Toast upon a
Milestone Birthday of
a Gentleman Friend

"Frank, as we raise a glass together to celebrate this monumental day, I can't help but thank my lucky stars, the good Lord above, and your mom and dad for one incredible tennis partner, but more than that—for one incredible best friend.

"Happy birthday, Frank. Here's to many, many more."

A Gentleman Does Not Say:

"Frank, the way you've lived, who would have thought you'd make it to fifty?"

A Toast upon a Milestone Birthday of a Lady Friend

"Julie, you make this evening beautiful, just as you make every day of our lives beautiful. It has been my honor to be your friend and to have shared the pleasure of your company through these truly wonderful years. I raise my glass to salute you, for all the good things that you do, and for the beauty you bring into the world."

A Gentleman Does Not Say:

"Julie, with the way you look, who would think you were fifty?"

A Toast Honoring a Friend upon His or Her Graduation

"Babs, it's a special honor to be included in this important moment in your life. All of your friends are fully aware of how hard you've worked. In fact, some of us may even feel that *we're* the ones qualified to go to work as chemical engineers.

"We are so very proud of you, and we all plan to stand back in admiration now as you shoot to the top of your new profession.

"Babs, here's to you."

A Gentleman Does Not Say:

"Babs, one more degree and you will officially be a professional student—it's time for you to go to work."

A Toast Celebrating the Baptism, Christening, or Naming of a Child

"What a joyous day this is for Julia and Hugh, but what a happy day it is for the rest of us too. Not only have we witnessed the first celebration in the life of Paige Elizabeth Sims, but we have also been introduced to a new friend, whose life will now be a part of our own.

"We raise our glasses in honor of Paige. May all her days be filled with such brightness and joy."

A Gentleman Does Not Say:

"What I would have given for the cushy, privileged life this kid is going to have."

A Toast at a Bar or Bat Mitzvah

"Shelly, I know how hard you've worked to get ready for this important moment. And we are all so proud of you and the splendid job you did in leading this morning's service.

"Your mom and dad were glowing, but so were all of the rest of us who've known you since the day you were born.

"Your joy is our joy on this day. *L'Chaim.*"

A Gentleman Does Not Say:

"Shelly, looks like you hit pay dirt today."

A Gentleman Responds to a Toast

Whenever a toast is proffered in his honor, a gentleman accepts it as the good-intentioned gesture that it is. Although his fraternity brothers or his coworkers may have grown rowdier over the course of the evening, the gentleman resists every urge for one-upmanship. Instead, although everyone else at the table may have stood to toast him and say "Hurrah!" in his honor, a gentleman keeps his seat. When his friends are seated once again, a gentleman stands—immediately, since they may not take another sip from their glasses until he has had his say—and offers the most efficient response possible. He is never wrong to say simply, "Thank you, that was very kind," or at the most, "Thank you, Jim, you're very kind to say those nice words. May I say what an honor and pleasure it is for me to be with you here tonight."

A Gentleman's Friends
Join in a Toast

When a gentleman is honored with a toast, his friends wait until the ever-so-brief ceremony is completed and then lift their own glasses to the honoree. They need make no verbal response except to say, "To Larry," "To Mitzi," or "To Mitzi and Mim." A friend is always correct in adding his own hearty "Hear! Hear!"

Next they touch glasses ever so lightly with those persons sitting within convenient arm's reach. No matter how casual the party, once a toast has been offered, a gentleman never rises from his seat to clink glasses with a person at a distant corner of the table. It is helpful to remember that the person at the other end of the table has touched glasses with persons nearer him or her, and this pleasantry has been passed on down the table, glass to glass. A toast, after all, is a communal experience.

A Toast for Mother's Day

"Everybody has a mother, Mom, but you're the one I was lucky enough to be blessed with. And what I was blessed with was selfless devotion, unflinching support, and absolutely unswerving love.

"If other guys can say the same thing about their own mothers, I guess they feel as lucky as I feel today.

"I love you, Mom. Happy Mother's Day."

A Gentleman Does Not Say:

"Mom, I know I'm responsible for the majority of the wrinkles on your face, but you're still beautiful to me."

A Toast for Father's Day

"Thank you, Dad, for all the games of catch in the backyard, for all the help with the homework, for the keys to the car, and for that money you wired when I ran out of cash in Paris.

"You really didn't have to do all these things—a lot of guys aren't as lucky as I am. I'm glad you did, though, and today I want to say thank you.

"I love you, Dad. Happy Father's Day."

A Gentleman Does Not Say:

"When I was younger, I thought you didn't have a clue, but now that I'm older, I get it."

A Toast for Memorial Day

"I rise now to raise a glass in tribute to all the men and women over the centuries who have taught us to cherish the rights and freedoms with which we are blessed.

"Theirs is the example of devotion, determination, and dedication to which we all should aspire. On this day we honor them for their willingness to make the ultimate sacrifice in order to assure those rights and freedoms for all of us and for all generations to come.

"To those whom we remember by name, and to those whose names we have never heard, let us raise our glasses in humility and thanks."

A Gentleman Does Not Say:

"Here's to a great holiday and an excuse to drink beer and go shopping."

A Toast for the Fourth of July

"Let's raise a glass to our country. May we never take for granted the blessings and freedoms that come to us as a birthright. Let us continue to do our best to extend those blessings to men and women everywhere, knowing that freedom is the birthright of all humankind.

"Here's to the United States of America and to a happy Fourth of July."

A Gentleman Does Not Say:

"Here's to the Fourth of July and a paid day off."

A Toast at
Thanksgiving Dinner

"Today, let us count our blessings and not our calories. Happy Thanksgiving to us all."

A Gentleman Does Not Say:

"I'm thankful that my evil ex-wife found one drop of kindness in her heart and allowed my kids to join us here today."

A Toast at Christmas Dinner

"This is a season of joy, a season of giving and receiving. There is no greater gift we can give one another than the joy of being together at this time of love and laughter. Simply by being together at this table, the best gift is already unwrapped. We give and we receive.

"Merry Christmas to us all."

A Gentleman Does Not Say:

"Even with the raw turkey, this has been a pretty good Christmas. Thank goodness Pizza Hut delivers on holidays."

A Toast for New Year's Eve

"I can't think of a better way to ring in the new year than with a group of people who have been such an important part of my past and, if the heavens are smiling on me, will be an equally important part of my future.

"Here's hoping the new year will bring each of us good health and happiness."

A Gentleman Does Not Say:

"Here's to the new year—it can't be any worse than the last one."

The Gentleman as Toastmaster

From time to time a gentleman may be asked to serve as toastmaster or master of ceremonies on a celebratory occasion. A gentleman feels honored that he has been entrusted to oversee the most festive part of the evening, but he also understands that his job is not one to be taken lightly. He knows that all too easily such an occasion can deteriorate into an open mike night, with every guest expecting to have his or her chance to share memories, either sentimental or sordid.

With the permission of his host or hostess, and well before the night of the party, a gentleman toastmaster plans the sequence of toasts and alerts each toast-giver to his or her place on the agenda. He also suggests to each toast-giver that his or her tribute should last no longer than five minutes.

The Teetotaller at Toasting Time

Many people, for any number of reasons, choose to abstain from drinking alcohol in any form. That decision, however, does not mean they must abstain from the tradition of raising a glass in honor of a good friend, beloved family member, or treasured coworker.

While it is considered bad form—and perhaps even bad luck—to toast with an empty glass, a gentleman feels perfectly comfortable raising a glass half-filled with whatever beverage he chooses. If he chooses to do so, merely in honor of the moment, he may ask that a little wine be poured in his glass so that he may raise his glass and touch it to his lips at the time of the toast. But even that bit of gamesmanship is unnecessary. If a gentleman does not drink alcohol, he feels no pressure to pretend otherwise.

A Housewarming Toast

"Tracey and Gus, as we gather here in this wonderful house, a dream you have worked long and hard to make come true, we wish you a long future of warm winters, flower-filled springs, tree-shaded summers, and red-and-gold autumns. And may this home always be filled with love, peace, and joy for you both, and for all who enter here."

A Gentleman Does Not Say:

"Tracey and Gus, what a great house! It obviously cost a fortune."

A Toast to Welcome a New Religious Leader

"Mary Ann, we know that you have been called to us with a sense of mission. We, too, are called—to be your coworkers, your helpers, and your friends. With you as our rabbi, we know Congregation Emmanuel is headed for even greater service to our community and to the world."

A Gentleman Does Not Say:

"We welcome you, Mary Ann—and as long as you keep your sermons short, you'll be with us for a long time."

A Toast upon a Religious Leader's Retirement

"Father O'Reilly, I know you think of us all as your children. You presided at our baptisms, our confirmations, and at so many of our weddings. At all those times, the celebrations were about us. Now the celebration is about you, and like grateful children, we give you our thanks and our love and we say, 'Come back soon, Father.' We know the house isn't going to be the same without you."

A Gentleman Does Not Say:

"Father O'Reilly, we are thankful for all you have done for us—but most of all for staying out of the wine cellar."

A Toast to Welcome a New Boss

"Jan, you've bravely chosen to join us. Please know that we intend to support you, realizing that creative ideas and imaginative strategies are the hope of the future. Here's to great days for you and even greater days for Corduroy Concepts."

A Gentleman Does Not Say:

"Jan, we are happy you are here, and if you last longer than our previous boss, we'll be even happier."

A Toast upon a Boss's Retirement

"Gary, the past seventeen years have been wonderful for Parity, Inc. Under your leadership the company has grown and flourished and taken the place it so rightly deserves in the Wisterville community. But these have also been wonderful years for me, as you've helped me, like so many others, grow and come to understand my true potential. You are a great leader, but I also consider you a great mentor and a friend.

"You have all my best wishes for many sunlit days on that sailboat of yours. The next time I see you, I expect you to be aglow from the Caribbean sun. Here's to you."

A Gentleman Does Not Say:

"You lucky dog, you are getting out of here while the rest of us will be sweating it out every day. I guess that's one good thing about getting old. Here's to you."

A Toast from a Boss Relinquishing His Position to His Successor

"Jim, I stand here to pass along to you the great responsibility entrusted to me ten years ago. I have given Gator Graphics my best. I believe you know that your best is what this company deserves. I salute you, knowing that your best is the very best possible. I hope to stand amazed as you lead us on to new heights we have not yet imagined."

A Gentleman Does Not Say:

"Jim, I know you can do this job, but just in case you find yourself in over your head, I'm a phone call away."

A Toast from a New Boss in Tribute to His Predecessor

"When Augusta Milbank called me, asking if I'd be interested in coming to Rolofson's, I jumped at the chance. Then, when I realized that she was talking about my succeeding Marvin Gosemark, I said to myself, 'What can you possibly be thinking? The man is a legend.' But I've also learned that he is one of the warmest people I've ever met.

"Thank you, Marvin, for all you've done to make Rolofson's the premier manufacturer of western saddles. It's my challenge to maintain your standards and my intention to maintain your traditions."

A Gentleman Does Not Say:

"I'm going to need everyone's help and prayers if I'm expected to clean up this mess I've inherited."

A Toast to Welcome a
New Coworker

"Marjorie, this is your first day among us. It's a pleasure to have you with us, and we look forward to knowing you and welcoming the fresh energy you bring to Keen Footwear.

"Let me say, 'Welcome,' and I know that everyone here at this moment will join me in saying 'Welcome' too."

A Gentleman Does Not Say:

"I don't know what kind of insanity you're suffering from that made you come to work here, but we are glad you did."

A Toast upon a Coworker's Retirement

"Paolo, I still recall the first time we ever met. It was my first day here at the firm, and you were the first person who spoke to me—except maybe for the guy in the elevator, who told me to turn right to find the men's room. I can remember your first words to me: You walked up to my desk, just after I'd taken off my jacket, and said, 'I'm Paolo. We're out of coffee. Come on, I'll show you how to make it so that Gertrude won't yell at you.'

"That's the kind of practical, useful guidance a fellow needs on his first day on the job. And it's the sort of advice, assistance, and guidance you give every day. Your presence hasn't just made this a better firm. It's also made it a better place to work. And it's made the rest of us better folks.

"Paolo, I just want to say thanks for everything."

A Gentleman Does Not Say:

"Paolo, I wish it were me and not you."

A Toast upon the Opening of a New Business

"Benchley, I know this is a day you've been looking forward to for years now. Now the signs are up and the doors are open.

"What lies ahead is greatness and a nationwide chain of Maple Burger franchises within the next five years.

"Please know how proud we all are of your accomplishments. Congratulations. You deserve every bit of the best."

A Gentleman Does Not Say:

"When times get tough and you're wondering what in the world made you quit the law firm and open a burger joint, your friends are all behind you."

A Toast upon the Happy Closing of a Business

"For over thirty years now, Frankie, Crosstown Gifts has been a part of all our lives. My parents bought my first teddy bear at your shop, and just last month I bought my new nephew's first teddy bear from you.

"I'm going to miss the chance to simply stop in and browse among all the wonderful items you were able to find, and I'm going to miss the chance to sit down with you late on a Saturday afternoon for one of our impromptu cups of coffee.

"Please know how many good memories you've given all of us. We love you and wish you all the best."

A Gentleman Does Not Say:

"I expect an invitation to that condo in Boca I helped you buy with all the money I spent here."

A Toast upon the Not-So-Happy Closing of a Business

"Elbert, we're gathered here tonight to honor you as you stand on the brink of your next adventure. We salute you as a friend, a man of integrity, and a man of vision.

"I am proud to call you my friend. I'm sure everyone here joins me in wishing you great and good things."

A Gentleman Does Not Say:

"I hate those mass merchants. People will realize what a great store this was once it's gone."

A Toast Honoring the Host or Hostess at an At-Home Dinner Party

"Sam [or Samantha], thank you so much for this lovely evening. I'd just like to say that you've outdone yourself once again.

"Here's to the heartiness of your hospitality and to this wonderful gathering of friends."

A Gentleman Does Not Say:

"Sam, this was a great party, even with the burned bread. It takes a pro to be able to rise above that."

A Toast Honoring the Host or Hostess of a Restaurant Dinner Party

"Lars [or Lorene], before we get much further into this evening, I'd like to propose a toast to say thank you for this splendid event. It's an honor to be here, among such good friends gathered in this beautiful setting.

"Thank you for making it happen. It's already a night to remember.

"We raise our glasses to you."

A Gentleman Does Not Say:

"Lars, thanks for such a great evening and for picking up the check."

Toasting in a Restaurant

Many restaurants boast of their care
and coddling of "private parties," but a
gentleman knows that in a public restaurant
no event is ever entirely private, even if it
is held in a room completely separate from
the main dining area.

Nevertheless, a gentleman knows that
dinner in a fine restaurant is an excellent,
and generous, way to celebrate a special
moment, mark a milestone, or simply
treat himself to the company of his most
cherished friends. When it comes time for
the toasting to begin, and especially if the
gentleman's party is seated at a table in
the main dining room, both the host and
his gentlemanly guests attempt to maintain
at least some decorum. The other diners
will most likely understand and appreciate
the fact that the host's party is a company
of devoted friends and relations, but they
will not appreciate having their own quiet
dinners interrupted by a marathon display
of toast-giving one-upmanship.

In such a situation, the host and his
guests may choose to deliver their toasts
without actually rising to their feet, and

they make a special effort to resist the temptation to let their toasts wander on as if they were after-dinner speeches. In short, they do their best to keep their intimate celebration as intimate as possible.

Likewise, well-behaved guests at nearby tables feel no urge to invite themselves, or insert themselves, into a celebration intended solely for the gentleman and his guests.

A Toast by a Host, in Tribute to a Friend Who Is Guest of Honor

"Leo, I've asked all these fine folks to join us this evening because I know they all share my love and respect for you. It's as simple as that. To be in your company is plenty of an excuse for a party.

"Permit us all to raise a glass in your honor, as generous soul, great friend, and one of the best golfers on the planet."

A Gentleman Does Not Say:

"Leo, I'm a little drunk, but I'd like to raise a glass to a great friend—my best friend. I love you, man."

A Toast by a Host in
Tribute to a Dignitary
Who Is Guest of Honor

"My friends, let me ask you to join me now in a toast to our guest of honor, a woman who has paved the way for so many others as a leading light in the field of international diplomacy. In more than thirty years of service to our nation, she has set new standards of integrity, patience, and determination, and her eloquence and composure under fire are the stuff of legend.

"Let us lift our glasses, then, to one of the great women of our generation: Ambassador Evelyn Kalko Early."

A Gentleman Does Not Say:

"I may not agree with your politics, but I'm honored to be in your presence."

A Toast in Honor of an Out-of-Town Guest

"All of you know that I've asked you to join me this evening so you can meet and share the company of my good friend, Malcolm Zachery. Ever since we met last year at the antique show in Dallas, I've been trying to get him to visit Pondbrook, just so I could introduce him to all of you.

"So I hope you will join me in saying welcome to Malcolm this evening, not just as a friend of mine but as a new friend of yours too. Malcolm, here's to you."

A Gentleman Does Not Say:

"Malcolm, I'm pleased to introduce you to my friends—and I'm especially glad that they got cleaned up and are on their best behavior."

A Toast by a Candidate for Public Office upon the Completion of a Successful Campaign, in Tribute to His Supporters and Staff

"Last night was one of the most exciting nights in my life. Standing in front of that microphone, I had the opportunity to say thank you to some of you specifically at that time, but now I want to tell you how much each of you has meant to me over the past year. This has been a team effort. It's my intention to keep the pledges and promises that we have made on the campaign trail. And I know it's going to take teamwork to make that happen too.

"Here's to you, my friends, the heart and soul, the arms and legs, and the smiling face of this campaign."

A Gentleman Does Not Say:

"We showed 'em."

A Toast by a Candidate for Public Office upon the Completion of an Unsuccessful Campaign, in Tribute to His Supporters and Staff

"Last night was tough for all of us, but late in the evening I told Lola that what got me through it was looking out across that ballroom and seeing all of you there, just as you have been there throughout the campaign. There is no better campaign staff anywhere. We got out the message. We did the job.

"I appreciate the opportunity to have worked with each of you. So here's to you, my friends."

A Gentleman Does Not Say:

"I know that most of you will want to focus on all the lies my opponent told about me, but we have to show that we are bigger than he is and move on."

A Toast Congratulating a Candidate upon the Completion of a Successful Campaign

"Roderick, we're here not just to say congratulations but to say thank you for providing the right message at the right time for the people of our community.

"It has been an honor to be a part of this campaign. Please know that all of us appreciate the chance to have been part of this experience, and we all look forward to the great things, and great days, you have in store for our town."

A Gentleman Does Not Say:

"Roderick, now that you've won, we hope you won't forget all the promises you made to us. But don't worry, we won't let you."

A Toast in Tribute to a Candidate upon the Completion of an Unsuccessful Campaign

"Roscoe, I know I speak for everyone under this tent when I say thank you. Running for office, especially in the way you did it—tirelessly, diligently, and graciously—is in itself a form of public service.

"We are all grateful to have been part of your campaign, and we look forward to standing beside you in your next step in life.

"My friends, here's to Roscoe Gaines, still the right man for the job."

A Gentleman Does Not Say:

"Roscoe, I'd like to invite you to have a drink with me a year from now so we can laugh at what a mess your opponent has made of the mayor's office."

A Toast Celebrating an Award
or Honor Received by a Friend

"All of us were watching 'the Maxxies' last Thursday night, Beryl, when your name was called. There were a lot of happy tears all over town that evening because so many of us know that this award isn't just about your skill as a set designer. It's also about the work you do every day to make the world a better place.

"Nobody deserves this honor more. Please know that we are proud—as we have always been—to be your friends."

A Gentleman Does Not Say:

"Nobody deserves this more, and just think, I remember when that set you built in high school came crashing down and you cried like a little girl."

A Toast in Honor of an Outstanding Achievement

"Last year around this time, Roy, nobody knew if Mallory Medical Center was going to make it. Then you stepped up to the plate and said, 'What we need is an effective annual campaign.' And you didn't just say it—you did it.

"Without your determination, your energy, and your refusal to take no for an answer, who knows where the children served by this hospital might be today? Now we know that Mallory will be here for them in the future as well.

"Because you have given them that assurance, we lift our glasses to you."

A Gentleman Does Not Say:

"I don't know if everyone here knows how much your family had to give up so that you could realize this dream, but they should. Here's to your tunnel vision."

A Toast in Recognition of a Heroic or Courageous Act

"Marilyn, we gather here to thank you, not just for your brave deeds, or your alertness in time of trouble, or your willingness to rise to the call of the moment. We also gather here to thank you for reminding us that the human spirit is a wondrous creation. And we thank you for being such a grand embodiment of that spirit."

A Gentleman Does Not Say:

"Marilyn, I didn't think you had it in you."

A Toast in Memory of a Great Friend or Benefactor

"Everett Elms is with us tonight in many ways: in the presence of his wife and children, in the company of his many friends and admirers, and in the many magnificent gifts he bestowed to worthy causes across our city.

"Let us raise our glasses in his memory, in gratitude for all he taught us and for the example he set. He was a joyful man, and his joy lives on.

"To Everett."

A Gentleman Does Not Say:

"To Everett. I know his wife won't mind my saying this, but that man could drink everyone here under the table and still embarrass us on the tennis court."

A Toast at a Wake or a Funeral Reception

"How splendid it is, I think, to come together here to remember Anthony. Here is the place where he spent so many hours and shared with so many of us the rich and lustrous stories of his life.

"This place will not be the same without him, but it remains enriched by his spirit, his jollity, his goodness, and his concern for his fellow man. All of that is embedded in the walls here.

"To these very walls, then, and to the memory of our dear friend Anthony, let us lift a glass."

A Gentleman Does Not Say:

"Let's lift a glass to Anthony. I'm sure that if he made it to heaven, he's looking down on us now and smiling."

When Those Creative Juices
Just Aren't Flowing . . .

The following classic toasts are appropriate for those occasions when a gentleman is at a loss for words.

"Here's looking at you." (from
   Casablanca)
"A toast to my best friend, _____,
   the richest man in town." (from *It's a
   Wonderful Life*)
"Cheers!"
"All the best."
"To your health."
"*L'Chaim*." (Hebrew for "to life")

Did I Really Say That?

Here are a few more simple toasts, ones that might have been considered amusing at some point in time. A gentleman does his best to avoid such tastelessness.

"Live long and prosper." (from *Star Trek*)

"My advice to you is to start drinking heavily." (from *Animal House*)

"Here's mud in your eye."

"Here's to good friends. Tonight is kind of special."

"Over the lips, past the gums, look out stomach, here it comes."

Classic Irish Toasts

No one has mastered the art of the toast like the Irish. Here are a few memorable quotations a gentleman might want to commit to memory for special occasions.

"May there be a generation of children on the children of your children."

"Here's to health, peace, and prosperity. May the flower of love never be nipped by the frost of disappointment, nor shadow of grief fall among your family and friends."

"May you be poor in misfortune, rich in blessings, slow to make enemies, and quick to make friends, and may you know nothing but happiness from this day forward."

"May your home always be too small to hold all your friends."

"We drink to your coffin. May it be built from the wood of a hundred-year-old oak tree that I shall plant tomorrow."

"May the good Lord take a liking to you—but not too soon!"

"There are good ships,
And there are wood ships,
The ships that sail the sea.
But the best ships are friendships,
And may they always be."

"May you be in heaven a full half-hour before the
   devil knows you're dead."
"May you live as long as you want and never want
   as long as you live."

> *"May neighbours respect you,*
> *Trouble neglect you,*
> *The angels protect you,*
> *And heaven accept you."*

Here's to You,
Wherever You Are

Toasts From Foreign Lands

A gentleman does not attempt to use foreign phrases unless he is truly comfortable doing so. Nevertheless, if he practices a bit a little while ahead of time, he may be able to join in the festivities by lifting a glass, with all good wishes, in almost any language.

Country	Traditional Toast
Argentina	¡Salud!
Australia	Cheers!
Austria	Prosit!
Belgium	Geluch!
Brazil	Saúde!
Canada	À votre santé!
China	Wen lei!
Columbia	¡Salud!
Czech Republic	Na zdravi!
Denmark	Skaal!
Egypt	Fee sihetak!
England	Cheers!
France	À votre santé!
Germany	Prost!
Greece	Eis igian!
Hong Kong	Gan bei!
Hungary	Kedves egészségére!
Iceland	Samtaka nu!

India	Aap ki sehat ue liye!
Ireland	Sláinte!
Israel	L'chaim!
Italy	Salute!
Japan	Omedeto gozaimasu!
Mexico	¡Salud!
Morocco	Saha wa afiab!
Monte Carlo	À votre santé!
The Netherlands	Proost!
New Zealand	Kia ora!
Norway	Skaal!
Philippines	Mabuhay!
Portugal	A sua saúde!
Russia	Za nas!
Scotland	Shlante!
South Africa	Gesondheid!
South Korea	Gun bae!
Spain	¡Salud!
Sweden	Skaal!
Switzerland	À votre santé!
Thailand	Sawasdi!
Venezuela	¡Salud!

A GENTLEMAN
PENS A NOTE

Saying "I'm sorry" or "thank you" should be the
simplest task in the world, but it is not. Instead it
is one of the most fearsome challenges faced by
gentlemen in today's complex, less-than-mannerly,
less-than-thoughtful society.

A gentleman will be greatly assisted, however,
by remembering a few rules that always remain the
same. It is never wrong to write a note, especially if it
is written on good cardstock. There are even instances
when a tastefully worded e-mail can be the way to
go. It is never wrong to say, via almost any form of
communication, "Congratulations to you," "Sorry
about the death of your mother," "Best wishes on your
upcoming nuptials," "Wasn't that a *great* party?" or
"I really look forward to using my new multi-pop-up
toaster."

Still, far too often a man views the writing of
a thank-you note, a sympathy note, or a note of
congratulation as a woeful obligation. He might better
consider his thank-you note as the completion of a
lovely evening, or even a continuance of a wonderfully
fulfilling experience. Similarly, his sympathy note can

well be seen as his expression of concern for a close friend who is grieving, or his acknowledgment of the death of a personal mentor, a beloved friend, a civic leader, or even a benefactor or volunteer who has made the world a better place.

His challenge is always to find the right words— and to identify the moments when he should write them. He always tries to write a note that will not embarrass him, but deep in his heart he can be confident that, if he thinks to write any note at all, he has already made it clear that he knows what kindness, consideration, and gratitude are all about.

A gentleman realizes that the moment he feels the urge to write a note about anything is the moment when he should pick up his pen.

THANK-YOU NOTES

A Thank-You Note for a Gift Happily Received

Dear Jesse,

    You know how much I love good, simple wine glasses. When I opened your package the other night, I was reminded of your good taste and your unfailing generosity. Very soon, when I use these glasses, I intend to make a toast to you.

    Sincerely,

    Phil

A Gentleman Does Not Write:

"Who knew you had such good taste?"

A Thank-You Note for a Gift
That You Really Don't Care For

Dear Gene and Ginger,

How could you have known that I'm thinking about taking golf lessons? Your set of monogrammed tees will be a real inspiration to me as I head for the course. Please know that I'm going to save them until I won't do them too much damage.

Thank you so much for being part of my birthday party.

Sincerely,

Granger

A Gentleman Does Not Write:

"Thanks. It's certainly not anything I'd ever have thought of buying for myself."

A Thank-You Note for a Holiday Gift When a Gentleman Has Not Given a Gift in Return

My Dear Gladys,

It was such a surprise to see you on my doorstep the day before Christmas, and you were so kind to give me the swim goggles. I'm looking forward to wearing them on my trip to Bali. It was so good of you to think of me in this way.

Wish we could see each other more often. Let's try to rectify that in the New Year.

I hope your holidays were great. Just seeing you made mine special.

Much love,

Rollo

A Gentleman Does Not Write:

"I wish I'd known you were getting me something."

A Thank-You Note for an At-Home Dinner Party

Dear Mary Sue,

Saturday night's dinner party was a truly lovely occasion. You always manage to attract such an interesting mix of people, and the dinner was a veritable feast. I particularly love white chocolate, so the dessert almost made me shout for joy.

Thanks, too, for seating me next to Kathy. I loved getting to hear about her work with songwriters, and as it turns out, we're both from Kentucky.

Only you could make this kind of evening happen.

All my best,

Russ

A Gentleman Does Not Write:

"I'm sure the food was delicious—I should have told you I'm allergic to shellfish."

A Thank-You Note for Dinner at a Restaurant

Dear Oscar,

You were great to include me in dinner last night at The Beaver's Paw. I had read so many great reviews of the place—both the food and the service.

Last night certainly lived up to my every expectation. In fact, The Paw may now be on my really short list of favorite bistros in town.

It's always a pleasure to be in your company. You really are one of the best hosts on the planet.

Thanks for a wonderful, memorable evening.

All my best,

Boris

A Gentleman Does Not Write:

"For such an inexpensive place, the food was pretty good."

A Thank-You Note for a Dinner Party That Did Not Go So Well

Dear Jessica,

It's always a pleasure to be in your presence, even when the gas jets aren't working. You were so smart to go ahead and bring in the pizza. Sitting around the living room, even with our overcoats on, we had the greatest time trying to distinguish the pepperoni from the veggie sausage.

With the help of Jack's wine cellar, we certainly persevered. You are a trouper. And it was fun to discover what troupers all of us can be—when we're having a really wonderful time.

Thanks so much,
Alfred

A Gentleman Does Not Write:

"I guess you'll remember to pay the gas bill next time."

A Thank-You Note for a Gift Written Long After the Fact

Dear Tracey and Hank,

This very morning I was drinking my cocoa from one of the funny "Kats R Kurious" mugs you gave me last Hanukkah. I still remember what fun I had just opening the package. Trust me, every time I use one of them—especially the one with the cat attempting to get the fireman down from the tree—I still laugh out loud.

Thanks for giving me such continuing pleasure.

Hope all is well with you and the boys.

Sincerely,

Izzy

A Gentleman Does Not Write:

"I'm so sorry this note is so late. I must be getting Alzheimer's."

A Thank-You Note for a Dinner Party Written Long After the Fact

Dear Brendan,

Yesterday while I was out for my midday run, I passed Kelly's Pub, where I could already smell the hickory smoke from the grill. Just that experience took me back to your cookout on Labor Day, and all the fun of it came back to me—especially your own perfectly smoked ribs.

Thanks for giving me such a great memory.

Best wishes,

Tom

A Gentleman Does Not Write:

"You'll have to forgive me, but I have been too busy to write."

A Thank-You Note After Being a Houseguest

Dear Loretta and Ron,

What fun it was getting to spend time with you in your beautiful condo this past weekend. It was great to wake up every morning and smell that fresh coffee brewing.

You were so kind to introduce me to your friends and to show me the sights in Bankersville. The new RollerDome is a marvel.

Best of all, however, was the time we had to relax and enjoy one another's company.

I hope you'll come visit Rockwart sometime soon. Say hi to the puppies for me.

Thanks so much,

Joe

A Gentleman Does Not Write:

"Your home was so clean—you must have hired a maid before I arrived."

A Thank-You Note for an Extraordinary Kindness

Dear Johnny,

You were so noble to help me through a tough time last week while I was stuck without a car. Those were especially busy days for me, and I don't know exactly what I would have done if you hadn't been so generous in letting me borrow the Honda.

Please know how much I appreciate your readiness to help a guy through a tough spot. Now that the Bentley's back up and running, let's go have a drink some time soon. I'll give you a buzz.

All my thanks.

Sincerely,

Ben

A Gentleman Does Not Write:

"Here's ten dollars for the gas I used. You can check the mileage if you want to."

A Thank-You Note for a Job Interview

Dear Ms. Longstray,

It was a pleasure to meet with you this afternoon. I appreciated the chance to learn more about Longstray and Bailey. I was especially interested to hear about your expansion in the fields of foliage retrieval and mulch creation.

Everything I heard today certainly reaffirms my thinking that Longstray and Bailey is a place where I could make a real contribution. I look forward to continuing our conversation and will stay in touch with Ms. Pebbly in Human Resources. Thanks so much for your time.

Sincerely yours,

Albert Josenblick

A Gentleman Does Not Write:

"I really want this job, and—assuming you can pay me what I'm worth—I will probably take it."

When Not to Write a Note

There are very rare instances when a gentleman may find it permissible, or even wise, not to write a note.

For example, he does not write a thank-you note for dinner parties or other occasions that are fund-raisers, either for charity or for political causes. Because he was present as a result of having written a check, he was in a very real way helping to throw the party. Therefore, no thank-you is required. (On the other hand, if an event has been particularly well produced, he may wish to dash off a congratulatory note to the people who made it happen.)

Neither does he feel driven to write a note for an everyday kindness, such as a friend's offering to buy him a soda, giving him a ride to the airport, or proofreading his section of the office annual report. Because there is really no such thing as an "everyday" kindness, however, a gentleman still makes a point of saying thank you and offering to return the favor when his help is needed.

What is more, a gentleman may find himself in situations where he would just as soon leave no written record of the experience. Confronted with an unfair accusation of rudeness, unfaithfulness, or unfairness, for example, he is best advised not to put his response (much less his emotions) on paper. He is best advised to handle such unpleasant situations in person, not even by means of telephone or (even worse) voice mail. He may discover far too late that his words have been recorded, making them every bit as problematic as if he'd written them down in his best blue-black ink.

In extremely difficult or complex situations, a gentleman lets his attorney do the writing.

Being Nice on the Net

The vast world of the social network is a part of almost every gentleman's life. Even though traditional good taste still demands that he send along a hand-written note to mark any of life's highly ceremonial or deeply solemn occasions, such as the wedding of a friend or the death of the loved one of a friend, a gentleman still can incorporate e-mailing into his well-mannered life.

As a quick rule of thumb, a gentleman finds it appropriate to send an e-mail to handle any communication that he might otherwise take care of by means of a phone call. For example, an e-mail saying "Thanks for drinks last night. It was fun being with you," or "Thanks for the ride to the airport. You're a lifesaver," is every bit as thoughtful as—and perhaps more thoughtful than—a message left in voice mail. A brief, to-the-point e-mail is also a correct response to any invitation that was itself sent via the internet.

A gentleman may also choose to express his joy upon the news of a happy occasion or his sadness at a friend's loss by sending a brief, but scrupulously worded, e-mail. He may say, "So glad to hear about the impending nuptials" or "I've just heard about your mother's death. Please know you are in my thoughts." Once again, in such cases, an e-mail may actually trump a phone call, since it does not intrude into the life of a friend who may either be tied up in wedding plans or disconcerted with grief.

In such instances, however, a gentleman knows that the e-mail does not complete his to-do list. He must follow up with a hand-written note, as soon as he possibly can, lest it appear that he is being dismissive of his friend's joy or sadness.

5 Occasions When an E-Mail Note is the Right Thing

1. To thank a friend for drinks at the bar or for a casual lunch or dinner
2. To thank a friend for a kindness, such as providing a ride to the airport, the auto shop, or the doctor's office
3. To thank a friend for an unexpected, but particularly thoughtful, compliment
4. To congratulate a friend on a new job, or a promotion
5. To thank a friend for congratulating you on a new job, or a promotion

5 Occasions When an E-Mail Note Is Not Enough

1. To thank a potential employer for a job interview
2. To say thank you for a wedding gift, no matter what it may have cost, and whether you like it or not
3. To say thank you after being a weekend guest in a friend's home
4. To express condolences for the death of the loved one of a friend
5. To express concern upon the loss of a job, or the foreclosure on a home

SYMPATHY NOTES, NOTES OF CONCERN, AND RESPONSES TO THEM

A gentleman knows that, in times of bereavement and trouble, the most honest, direct words are the best words possible. If he has been well acquainted with the person who has died, his note includes some mention of that person's good attributes or a remembrance of the person's kind treatment of the gentleman himself. ("I remember how welcoming your mother was, Jim, every time we'd come home, all covered in mud, after the football games in the park.")

On the other hand, if he did not actually know the deceased person, a gentleman may express his sympathies directly to his friend, saying, "Jim, I have heard about your mother's death. Please know that you are in my thoughts."

A gentleman may feel confident in writing a sympathy note upon the death of any good friend, close coworker, or acquaintance. He may also feel comfortable in expressing his sympathy to any friend or coworker who has lost a relative, a close friend, or even a cherished pet.

In such situations he need not be too specific in his condolences. Instead he is wise to focus on his relationship with his friend or coworker: "I've heard about Polly's death. I know she meant a great deal to you. Please know you are in my thoughts."

In some instances a gentleman may wish to extend condolences to several family members who do not live in the same household. In such cases, he may choose to send one well-worded note to one of the bereaved, adding at the end of the note, "I hope you will share my thoughts with Jim, Jack, Suzy, and Sam. I am thinking of you all at this time."

If a gentleman is a praying person, he may replace "you are in my thoughts" with "you are in my prayers."

A bereaved gentleman realizes that not only flowers sent in a time of concern, but also cards and kind words, should be acknowledged with a short note. This note does not have to be lengthy because a gentleman may have hundreds of such notes to write. A few short words are all that is required to let someone know that his or her gesture was sincerely appreciated.

A Sympathy Note to a Close Friend upon the Death of a Spouse or Life Partner

Dear Marianne,

I've just learned about Jim's death. It's hard for me to know what to say at this moment, but I do know that I remember all the great times we spent together (the two of you, with Ginny and me). He was generous of spirit, in all things.

Ginny and I have always admired the warmth and camaraderie of your relationship. I know you will miss him. So will Ginny. And so will I.

Please know that you are in our thoughts.

Sincerely,

Ted

A Gentleman Does Not Write:

"I know exactly what you are going through. When I lost Sally . . ."

A Sympathy Note upon the Death of a Business Acquaintance or the Death of a Coworker's Relative

Dear Tom [or "Mr. Gruston"],

Just today Sibbley Clark told me about Jennifer's [or "Mrs. Gruston's"] death. Although I did not know her well, I admired her presence in the business community and her many good works as a community volunteer. Here in the office, it always made me happy to hear about your shared devotion to your family.

Please know that my thoughts ["and Mary Sue's," if applicable] are with you at this time.

Sincerely,

Otto [or "Otto Bailey"]

A Gentleman Does Not Write:

"It just goes to show you—we never know when we will be taken from this earth."

A Sympathy Note to a Friend or Coworker upon the Death of a Close Friend

Dear Harry,

I know how much Lester meant to you as a friend. I always enjoyed hearing you talk about your great times on your camping trips. Just listening to those stories, I got the sense that he was a fun guy and a really special person to you.

Just wanted you to know that I was thinking about you.

Sincerely,

Preston

A Gentleman Does Not Write:

"I know this is a hard time for you, but don't let this get you down."

A Sympathy Note upon the Death of a Child

Dear Esther and Eric,

    The news of Jessica's death fills me with great sadness. I have always admired your family for its closeness and the warmth you have so clearly shared.

    Please know that you are in my thoughts.

    Sincerely,

    Houston

A Gentleman Does Not Write:

"It should give you some comfort to know that Jessica is in heaven."

A Sympathy Note upon the Death of an Infant or a Miscarriage

Dear Patty and Paul,

I have just heard of your loss. I will not attempt to find words to express my sadness, since there are no words that can handle this moment in anybody's life.

Please know, however, that I am thinking of you.

Sincerely,

Mike

A Gentleman Does Not Write:

"If there is anything I can do for you, please let me know."

A Sympathy Note to a Friend or Coworker upon the Death of a Beloved Pet

Dear Hallie,

I was really sad to learn about Mr. Bibbs's death. I know that he was one of your best pals, always accepting and ready to have fun.

As he got on in age, I truly admired the way you gave him the care and loving comfort that seemed right, in appreciation of the joy he had brought into your life.

Sincerely,

Barton

A Gentleman Does Not Write:

"You must have been expecting this—Mr. Bibbs was pretty old for a cat."

A Response to a Sympathy Note

Dear Otto,

    Your kind words were a great comfort in the wake of Maggie's death. These are tough times, but your support and concern are a true source of strength.

    Thank you so much for lending your support in this special way.

    Sincerely,

    Tom Gruston

A Gentleman Does Not Write:

"The bright side of this is that I now know how many people care for me."

A Note of Concern for a Friend's Health

Dear Edward,

I have heard the news about your diagnosis. There is no reason that this disease chooses to strike one person rather than another. You are, however, a brave, strong-willed fellow, and you have an army of friends to stick with you through the coming days.

Please know how honored I am to be one of that army.

You are in my thoughts.

Sincerely,

Peter

A Gentleman Does Not Write:

"I hope you will finally begin taking care of yourself—I don't want to lose you."

A Note of Concern for the Loss of a Job

Dear Ursula,

Jack told me today that you are no longer with Pacific Packaging. I know how much you enjoyed working for them, and I know how devoted you were to the company.

As you move toward your next adventure, please know that I, like so many others, will want to hear about your progress. Please know that we're there to support you.

I'll call you in the next few days, and we'll grab some lunch. Okay? I know this is probably a tough time. You are in my thoughts.

Sincerely,

Carlos

A Gentleman Does Not Write:

"If there is anything I can do for you—short of a loan—let me know."

A Note of Concern at the Breakup of a Relationship

Dear Chuck,

I'm so sorry to hear about you and Debra. I value you both as friends, and I regret that things are not working out. I know you both did your best to make your relationship work.

This is a difficult time, I'm sure, but I hope you'll let me and the rest of your friends provide the support that we're ready to offer.

I'll be in touch sometime later this week. Maybe we can grab a drink or shoot some hoops.

Sincerely,

Dennis

A Gentleman Does Not Write:

"I must admit—you stuck it out longer than I would have. I have got the perfect girl for you to meet. Just give me the word and I'll introduce you."

A Response to a Card or Letter of Concern

Dear Peter,

I hope you know how your kind words encouraged me during my stay in the hospital. The surgery hit me with a wallop that I hadn't expected, so I really valued the support of thoughtful friends like you.

Now that I'm back up and running—almost at full speed—I look forward to seeing you in the very near future. Many, many thanks.

Sincerely,

Edward

A Gentleman Does Not Write:

"Thank you for just sending a note and not coming to visit like everyone else. It seemed like every time I was about to get some rest, another person whom I had to entertain walked in."

A Gentleman and His Stationery

Since a gentleman may be called upon
to write a note, extend an invitation, or
dash off a few words of gratitude at any
moment, he makes sure that he always has
on hand a ready supply of writing paper and
envelopes, note cards, good-quality pens,
and postage.

The staples of his stationery stash will
include supplies of

- Monarch sheets (writing paper
  measuring 7 1/4 by 10 1/2 inches) in
  ecru, white, or pale gray. Monarch
  sheets, with their envelopes, may
  be used for personal or business
  correspondence. A gentleman may
  wish to have his name, along with his
  home address, engraved or printed
  at the top of each sheet. He will also
  want to have his address (without his
  name) added to the back flap of his
  envelopes.
- Correspondence cards (heavy-
  duty cards measuring 71/4 by 3 7/8
  inches) in ecru, white, or pale gray.
  Correspondence cards, which fit
  in the same envelopes as monarch

sheets, may be used for almost any personal correspondence—sympathy notes, thank-you notes, and even party invitations. A gentleman may wish to have his name—without his address—engraved or printed on each card.

- Enclosure cards (heavy-duty cards measuring 3 1/4 by 1 3/4 inches) in ecru, white, or pale gray. Also known as "calling cards," enclosure cards come with their own envelopes and are engraved or printed with the gentleman's full name. These cards are too small to be mailed through the U.S. Postal Service. They are invaluable, however, when a gentleman needs to write a brief note to accompany a gift or when he simply wishes to jot down a quick message to be attached to a newspaper clipping, a photograph, or a photocopy of another document.

- Postcards in any number of colors and illustrated in all sorts of amusing and interesting ways. Simply by picking up a few attractive cards whenever he is in a gift shop or visiting a museum, a gentleman

may accrue a collection of cards
that he can use for any impromptu
correspondence, including thank-you
notes for gifts and informal get-
togethers.

If a gentleman chooses to have his
stationery engraved, he will be wise to go
ahead and purchase his own solid brass
"die," including his full name and his home
address. The engraver can mask different
portions of the die during the engraving
process, so that the same die can serve for
any of a gentleman's stationery needs.

Because high-quality stationery is
not inexpensive, a gentleman may be well
advised to write a draft of any note that
he intends to send out on his personalized
cards and papers.

INVITATIONS
AND RESPONSES
TO THEM

When a gentleman invites friends, acquaintances, or coworkers to any occasion for which he is host, he makes sure he provides all the pertinent information in a clear, concise manner. He makes especially sure to include the time and location of the event, as well as some sort of explanation as to what sort of food and drink his guests may expect to find when they arrive. If he expects his guests to honor some sort of dress code, he makes sure it is clearly stipulated in his invitation. Even if he does not request that his guests "RSVP," he still includes a telephone number, since he knows that invariably somebody will need to call for directions.

A gentleman responds in a timely manner to any invitations he receives. Although most formal invitations include a response card, a gentleman should be able to compose an acceptance note if such a card is not included. For less formal occasions, a gentleman may either respond in writing or via phone.

Responses to very casual invitations are expected to be, and are most appropriately, returned by phone.

When a gentleman accepts an invitation via note or phone, he makes sure to mention the date and time at which he is expected to arrive, just so his host (or hostess) knows that he understands the game plan; when he declines an invitation he need not reiterate the details, since he does not plan to be present.

An Invitation to a Somewhat Formal Occasion

[Printed on a computer or at a print shop, or handwritten on plain stationery or a sturdy correspondence card.]

Mitchell Mullins

requests the pleasure of your company for

Cocktails

seven o'clock

Friday, August 27

8746 Ocean Drive, Apt. 4-P

998-3313

Coat and tie

An Invitation to a Casual Get-together

Dear Millie,

I'm asking a few people over for drinks on Friday, July 27, at seven o'clock. My friends Eddie and Abigail Jussworth will be in town for the weekend, and I want you to meet them.

We'll be very, very casual. I have a suspicion that Gil will be bringing his Twister game.

Please let me know if you can make it.

Looking forward to seeing you.

All best,

Mitch Mullins

998-3313

[Mitch will include his address on the outside of the envelope.]

A Gentleman Does Not Write:

"I will just be serving wine, so if you want anything stronger, BYOB."

The Most Casual Invitation Possible (Other Than a Phone Call)

I'm pouring Cosmos on Friday.

Don't come before 7. Don't come after 10.

Call me.

Mitch

998-3313

A Response to a Formal Wedding Invitation

[Handwritten on plain stationery or a sturdy correspondence card.]

Jonathan Hazelbirth

is pleased to accept

Mrs. Needly's kind invitation for

Saturday, October 1

at the Overbought Club

following the ceremony at St. Ustley's Church

[In this situation the gentleman is responding only to the invitation to the reception, not to the wedding ceremony. The reception is the social occasion. The wedding ceremony is a public church service and therefore is theoretically open to the entire community. Also note that a gentleman omits any punctuation at the line breaks. The line breaks themselves take the place of the punctuation.]

A Response Declining an Invitation to a Formal Wedding

Jonathan Hazelbirth

regrets that he is unable to accept

Mrs. Needly's kind invitation for

Saturday, October 1

A Written Response to a Somewhat Formal Invitation (such as Mitch Mullins's invitation for cocktails on page 111)

Dear Mitch,

    Thanks for the invitation for 7:00 p.m. on Friday the 27th. I'll be there and I'm looking forward to it.

    Thanks,

    Gary

A Written Response Declining a Somewhat Formal Invitation (such as Mitch Mullins's invitation for cocktails on page 111)

Dear Mitch,

I've received your invite for drinks on Friday the 27th. Unfortunately, I've already made plans to be in Gallville with my parents that weekend.

I know you'll have a great time. When I get back in town, I want to hear all about it.

Thanks so much for the invitation. I wish I could say yes.

Sincerely,

Gary

A Gentleman Does Not Write:

"I wish you had invited me earlier—before I went and bought theater tickets for that evening."

When to Use Titles

In the excruciatingly correct correspondence of excruciatingly correct society, the name of any person—whether on the front of an envelope, or in the salutation of a letter—must be preceded by a title. Honorific titles such as "Mr.," "Ms.," "Miss," or "Mrs." are used merely as a matter of courtesy. Professional titles such as "Dr.," "Senator," or "Reverend" are used in business correspondence that actually relates to the title-holder's job, as well as in social correspondence.

A gentleman is never wrong in using an honorific or a professional title in his personal correspondence. However, he may choose whether to use a title based on his familiarity with the recipient and the formality of the correspondence. When a gentleman writes a thank-you note to his neighbor, who is a dentist and a close friend, he may address the envelope to "James Morton" and begin the letter "Dear James." However, when he sends this neighbor a formal wedding invitation, he addresses it to "Dr. James Morton."

A gentleman takes the time to consult

an etiquette book or an appropriate Web site to determine the correct form of address and salutation for any clergyman, government official, college or university official, member of the military, or other professional with whom he wishes to correspond. He may also find this information in the reference section of many dictionaries. He thus knows, when writing a congratulatory note to his senator, to address the envelope to "The Honorable Julia Ferrelli" and to begin his letter with the salutation "Dear Senator Ferrelli."

Mr., Miss, Ms., or Mrs.?

These days a gentleman is well warned to take care in applying honorific titles such as "Mr.," "Miss," "Ms.," or "Mrs." without foreknowledge. If he receives, for example, a letter signed by "Karey Thompson," he may find himself in a dilemma, unsure whether to reply to "Mr. Thompson" or "Ms. Thompson." His best bet in such cases is simply to reply to "Karey Thompson," both on his return envelope and in the salutation at the head of the enclosed letter or note.

While a gentleman may feel secure at almost any time in referring to women correspondents as "Ms. Smith," "Ms. Jones," or "Ms. Zilliwitsch," he is wise to defer to the implied wishes of a woman who has signed her letter—or even identified herself on the return envelope—as "Miss Zilliwitsch" or "Mrs. Patrick K. Magursky."

NOTES OF CONGRATULATION

A gentleman rejoices in the successes of his friends. Since such moments in life are invariably happy, he seizes upon them to offer his good wishes and joyous support. He knows that he will be with his friends during the hard times, but he also knows that his thoughtfulness is more than welcome in the good times too.

When writing notes of congratulation to engaged friends, a gentleman naturally respects the tradition of offering his "best wishes" to the bride, while offering his "congratulations" to the groom. The tradition stems from the idea that it is the man who is lucky to have won the woman.

Even if his feelings regarding his friends' personal lives and accomplishments are not totally blissful, he knows that a note of congratulation is a little gift, not a chance to give a lecture. In such cases, if he feels that he cannot sincerely say he is happy with his friends' decisions, he is better off saying nothing at all. He knows, however, that whatever his personal standards or opinions, he does not impugn his own integrity by saying, "I wish you well."

A Note of Best Wishes upon an Engagement Announcement, Written to the Bride-to-Be

Dear Angela,

It was great to run into you and Bosco the other night and to hear your good news. If I may be so bold, I want it known that I've always said the two of you make a great couple.

You do know, don't you, that I met Bosco in junior high and that we've been great buddies ever since? I've told him over and over that great things were in store for him. Now I know my prediction has come true.

With all my best wishes,

Linus

A Gentleman Does Not Write:

"You snagged a good one."

A Note of Congratulation upon an Engagement Announcement, Written to the Groom-to-Be

Dear Bosco,

It made me happy to hear the great news about you and Angela. She is a wonderful woman. Good work, my friend.

I've told her how long we've known each other, but I didn't offer to tell her any tales from our days at Bixley High, especially the senior trip to DC. That's the kind of real buddy I am.

I hope you know that you have my honest and heartfelt congratulations.

With all my best,

Linus

A Gentleman Does Not Write:

"Angela seems like a great catch, but I'd get a prenup just in case (ha ha)."

A Note of Best Wishes to a Newly Married Couple

Dear Maddie and Gilbert,

I saw the announcement of your wedding in today's *Examiner*. What good news that is. I'm passing a copy along to my mom, who will remember my talking about you when we worked together at the law firm.

Both of you are great folks. Please know that you have my warmest good wishes.

Sincerely,

Toby Marquess

A Gentleman Does Not Write:

"Sounds like it was a wonderful wedding. Wish I had made the list."

A Note of Best Wishes to Be Enclosed with a Wedding Gift

Dear Maddie and Gilbert,

    I hope these champagne flutes will play a part in the many celebrations that are to come as the two of you begin your life together.

    With all my best wishes,

    Jack Walburn

[Jack, of course, writes his note on a heavyweight enclosure card. If he has a stock of enclosure cards already engraved or printed with his full name, he simply signs his note "Jack," or he may, even more simply, just strike through his last name, "Walburn," to make it clear that he considers himself to be on a first-name basis with the recipients.]

A Gentleman Does Not Write:

"If you don't like these, I got them at Giard Gifts. You can return them."

A Note of Congratulation to a Couple upon the Renewal of Their Marriage Vows

Dear Margaret and Fred,

It was an honor for me to be present as you renewed your wedding vows. It was a moving experience, not least of all because of the beautiful words each of you shared about your love.

And the reception was a pretty grand bash too. It was especially nice to be able to meet so many of your old friends.

With sincere good wishes,

Andy

A Gentleman Does Not Write:

"Fred, most of us are looking for a way out of the mistake we made twenty years ago, and here you are doing it again. You're a better man than I."

A Note of Congratulation upon the Birth of a Baby

Dear Ros and Mike,

I just heard the wonderful news that little Roslyn Michelle has arrived. I know the two of you must be exhausted, but I bet you can't tell whether it's from sleep deprivation or from sheer joy and the anticipation of all the great adventures that lie ahead of you and your little girl.

I want to be introduced to her sometime before too long, just as I look forward to congratulating the two of you in person.

All my best,

Flaven

A Gentleman Does Not Write:

"I can't wait to meet the little girl who made Mike miss so many poker games on Lamaze class nights."

A Note of Congratulation upon a Milestone Anniversary

Dear Whitney and Wally,

I read in the newspaper about the celebration of your forty years together. When I look at the two of you, I get a sense of how wonderful those years, and decades, have been. I am also proud to be able to have shared some of those good times in the warmth of your beautiful home.

It is my great honor to be your friend.

Please know that you have my sincere congratulations and my warmest best wishes.

Joy to both of you,

Zack Moberton

A Gentleman Does Not Write:

"Congrats on sticking it out this long. I know from my own experience that it isn't easy."

A Note of Congratulation upon a Friend's New Job

Dear Alex,

I hear you're starting at Douster & Sons next week. I know the company's reputation and understand that the people there are great folks.

They're also very smart if they've got the good sense to hire you.

Let's get together for lunch sometime, now that you're going to be working downtown.

Congratulations to you, and to the Dousters.

Sincerely,

Rick

A Gentleman Does Not Write:

"Now that you're making the big bucks, lunch is on you."

A Note of Congratulation upon a Friend's or Coworker's Retirement

Dear Eleanor,

On my very first day at the office, you were the very first person to offer a word of welcome. Actually, what I remember you saying is, "May I show you how to make the coffee?"

That's the kind of practical knowledge you've continued to impart. I remain so grateful for your counsel over the years.

Congratulations on your retirement, even though I'm missing you already.

Sincerely,

Nate

A Gentleman Does Not Write:

"Expect some calls from me asking you questions—you are the only one who knows how to do the quarterly report."

A Note of Congratulation upon the Recent Success of a Friend or Acquaintance

Dear Bono,

I saw your new CD in Disc-a-Thon yesterday. Frankly, I couldn't miss it, considering the size of the display.

When I took my copy to the register, three other people in line were buying copies too. That's the best news possible, I guess.

Isn't it great to see your hard work pay off? I look forward to saying, "I knew him when." In fact, I'm saying it already.

I'll be watching for you on the awards shows.

All my best,

Roger

A Gentleman Does Not Write:

"I hope being a star will be everything you hoped it would be."

How to Address an Envelope

When addressing an envelope, a gentleman's main goal is to make sure that his message reaches its recipient as expeditiously as possible. He attempts to write clearly, providing up-to-date address details and including his recipient's postal code—in every case. (In the United States, the five-digit zip code is obligatory, but a gentleman knows that adding the "plus-four" code may help ensure that his mail reaches its destination more smoothly.)

In social correspondence, the first line of a standard address includes the name of the recipient or recipients of the letter, along with any appropriate social or professional titles. The second line includes the street address, including any relevant apartment or suite number. The third line includes the city, state, and postal code to which the envelope is to be delivered. For example:

Mr. and Mrs. Joseph Grant

226 Gustavus Lane, Apartment A-6

Nashville, TN 37205-3932

The U.S. Postal Service requests that standard two-letter abbreviations be used for the fifty states (for example, "ME" for Maine or "WY" for Wyoming). However, a gentleman may choose to either spell out or abbreviate other standard elements of the address, according to his preference. He may use "Street" or "St.," "Avenue" or "Ave.," trusting that—if his penmanship is proficient—his envelope will reach its recipient in a timely manner.

If a gentleman has any reason to assume that his correspondence may be returned to him (or if he simply wants to make sure that his correspondent has the right information for getting in touch with him), he makes sure that his return address is included on any envelope he puts in the mail. He may choose to place his return address on the upper left-hand corner of the front of the envelope. Or he may place it on the flap on the back of the envelope. Either way he is correct. What is more, if an envelope must be returned, the Postal Service employees are trained to look in either spot for the sender's address.

NOTES OF APOLOGY AND RESPONSES TO THEM

A gentleman makes every effort to behave himself at all times and hopes never to give distress or displeasure to another person. Yet he remains—for all his good intentions—a fallible human being, which means that from time to time, and on what he hopes are infrequent occasions, he does screw up.

Because he is a gentleman, however, he attempts to straighten out the situation (and recoup his losses) as quickly as possible. He knows that, in most cases, apologies are best offered in person, or at least by telephone, since face-to-face communication may actually help calm the waters more easily. It may even give him a better insight into his affronted friend's side of the story.

If his friend or acquaintance is convinced that he or she has been severely insulted or that the gentleman has been intentionally rude or thoughtless, the gentleman may even be accused of cowardice for apologizing in writing. Nevertheless, some situations demand that a gentleman attempt to make amends by means of the written word.

Even if a gentleman feels that he has been misinterpreted or wrongly accused, he may find it noble to say, "I am sorry that my actions caused you unhappiness [or even "pain"]. I hope you know that I did not mean to give offense." He never turns an apology into an argument on his own behalf or a defense of his own behavior.

The only time a gentleman may correctly refuse to offer an apology is when he has been accused of rudeness when standing up for his ethical convictions or his political beliefs. Even then, however, if he has raised his voice to the point of bullying or if he has disrupted a dinner party by provoking an argument at the table, he may still find it necessary to say, "I'm sorry for letting my anger get the best of me."

Knowing how to say "I'm sorry" is a valuable skill, but it is not one that a gentleman wishes to hone by overuse. A gentleman is well advised to attempt at all times to live his life in a way that requires as few apologies as possible.

If a gentleman receives an apology in the form of a note, he must respond to that gesture in a timely manner. A note of acceptance of an apology should simply say the offending party is forgiven, so that life may get back to normal. A gentleman does not wait, hoping that he will run into Grace at a cocktail party where he can tell her he accepts her apology. He may not run into Grace anytime soon; more important, he would never open an old wound, especially in the midst of a happy occasion.

An Apology Note After Destroying a Piece of a Host's Heirloom China (or Any Other Valued Property)

Dear Agatha,

You were kind to be so gracious about my clumsiness at your wonderful dinner party on Saturday evening. I wish I had noticed the casserole coming across the table, but I didn't.

I hope you'll forgive me for being such an oaf.

Sincerely,

Percy

A Gentleman Does Not Write:

"Please accept this check for forty dollars for the salad plate I broke—I checked on eBay and that should cover it."

An Apology Note for Inappropriate Behavior

Dear Doris,

I realize now that I behaved rather badly at the reception following little Kaitlyn's christening. The truth of the matter is, I had way too much of the celebratory champagne. I hope you know that otherwise I would never have attempted to wear Kaitlyn's car seat on my head.

This was a day that should evoke only good memories in the future. Please forgive me if my behavior has marred those memories in any way.

Sincerely,

Randy

A Gentleman Does Not Write:

"If it makes you feel any better, I had the world's worst hangover the next morning."

An Apology Note for Having Missed a Business Appointment

Dear Mr. Grousehawk,

Please accept my apology for having missed our lunch appointment yesterday. After having been caught for more than an hour in the traffic jam caused by an accident, I did finally manage to contact your assistant, Ms. Tidwell, who told me you were obliged to proceed without me.

I understand the demands of your schedule, and I wish I could have alerted you sooner. I hope we will be able to reschedule a time to get together and discuss my proposal.

Sincerely,

Malcolm Habbyway

A Gentleman Does Not Write:

"Sorry about missing the appointment, but something came up that I couldn't get out of."

An Apology Note for Having Missed a Social Occasion

Dear Enrique,

I'm so sorry to have missed last night's dinner party. I was looking forward to it, and I was especially excited about having the chance to see Stephanie again.

Unfortunately, late in the afternoon I was hit with a twenty-four-hour bug of some sort. I'm only getting back up to speed right now, and it's five o'clock on Sunday.

I know the dinner was great. I regret having to miss a good time with so many great folks.

Sincerely,

Hiram

A Gentleman Does Not Write:

"I'm sorry I missed the party, but if I had been there I would have been upchucking all night."

An Apology Note to a Friend Who Feels He Has Been Insulted

Dear Arthur,

I fear that I hurt your feelings on Saturday evening when I mentioned your new hairpiece in front of the Leskies. It was not my intention to cause you any embarrassment, and I realize now that I should have been more careful about making this sort of remark—especially in front of people with whom you are not well acquainted.

I consider you a good friend, and I am sorry for having put you, and the Leskies, on the spot.

Please accept my sincere apology.

Yours truly,

Bill

A Gentleman Does Not Write:

"Sorry about the hairpiece remark. I always seem to put my foot in my mouth."

A Response to an Apology

Dear Bill,

Thank you for your note. You were good to send it.

I have to admit that the "new rug" remark did catch me a bit off guard, but I fully understand that you meant no harm. You are a friend and a person well known for his thoughtfulness and consideration for others.

I appreciate your writing. It has completely cleared the air, as far as I'm concerned.

Sincerely,

Arthur

A Gentleman Does Not Write:

"I accept your apology. Just don't let it happen again."

INDEX

note of best wishes
enclosed with
wedding gift, 125
thank-you note by
e-mail, 91
thank-you note for, 75,
76, 77
glassware, 4
raising, 6
graduation, of friend, 25
Greeks, and toast tradition,
18
groom-to-be,
congratulations to, 123
guest, toast to honor out-of-
town, 57
guest of honor
tribute to dignitary
as, 56
tribute to friend as, 55

H

health, note expressing
concern for friend, 102
heroic act, recognition of,
64
holiday toasts
Christmas dinner, 35
Father's Day, 31
Fourth of July, 33
Memorial Day, 32
Mother's Day, 30
New Year's Eve, 36
Thanksgiving dinner,
34
honor, friend's receipt of, 62
honorific titles, 118
host/hostess
honoring at at-home
dinner party, 51

honoring at restaurant
dinner party, 52
houseguest, thank-you note
after being, 83
housewarming, 39

I

inappropriate behavior,
apology for, 139
infant's death, sympathy
note to friend upon, 99
initiating toast, 7
insulting feelings of person,
apology for, 142
invitation responses,
109–110
declining wedding
invitation, 115
by e-mail, 88
to formal invitation, 116
to formal wedding
invitation, 114
written to decline
formal invitation, 117
invitations, 109–113
to casual get-together,
112
to formal occasion, 111
most casual, 113
Irish toasts, 69–70

J

job, congratulations on new,
129
job interview
e-mail insufficient for
thank-you, 91
thank-you note for, 85
job loss, note expressing
concern for friend, 103